Selecting, Managing, and Marketing Technologies

The Practicing Administrator's Leadership Series
Jerry J. Herman and Janice L. Herman, Editors

**ROADMAPS
TO SUCCESS**

Other Titles in This Series Include:

Selecting, Managing, and Marketing Technologies

Jamieson A. McKenzie

CORWIN PRESS, INC.
A Sage Publications Company
Newbury Park, California

For information address:

Corwin Press, Inc.
A Sage Publications Company
2455 Teller Road
Newbury Park, California 91320

SAGE Publications Ltd.
6 Bonhill Street
London EC2A 4PU
United Kingdom

SAGE Publications India Pvt. Ltd.
M-32 Market
Greater Kailash I
New Delhi 110 048 India

Printed in the United States of America

Library of Congress Cataloging-in-Publication Data

McKenzie, Jamieson A. (Jamieson Angus), 1945-
    Selecting, managing & marketing technologies / Jamieson A.
McKenzie.
        p.   cm. — (Roadmaps to success)
    Includes bibliographical references (p.   ).
    ISBN 0-8039-6054-9
        1. Educational technology—United States—Planning—Handbooks,
manuals, etc. 2. School management and organization—United States—
Handbooks, manuals, etc.   I. Title.   II. Title: Selecting,
managing, and marketing technologies.   III. Series.
LB1028.3.M395   1993
371.3'078—dc20   93-22349

93 94 95 96 10 9 8 7 6 5 4 3 2 1

Corwin Press Production Editor: Marie Louise Penchoen

Contents

Foreword

In *Selecting, Managing, and Marketing Technologies*, Jamieson A. McKenzie argues convincingly for a comprehensive approach to planning for and managing the use of technology in schools. He stresses the importance of (1) anticipating the future, (2) creating stakeholders' planning committees, (3) providing staff development and training for teachers and administrators, (4) winning community support by skilled marketing techniques, and (5) identifying and obtaining new sources of funding for the technology needs that exist in one's schools.

He provides specific steps to follow when dealing with vendors of technology, and he offers a series of guidelines for designing the staff development program for teachers and administrators.

McKenzie's Chapter 5, "Identifying New Sources of Funding for Technology," is especially helpful in these lean economic times. He ends by providing a series of appendixes that can be used by the reader to determine the level of technological understanding, planning, and usage that exists in schools.

JERRY J. HERMAN
JANICE L. HERMAN
Series Co-Editors

About the Author

Jamieson A. McKenzie is President of Network 609, an educational consulting firm in Nantucket, MA. Before becoming a full-time writer and consultant, he served in many administrative and teaching positions, including superintendent; assistant superintendent; elementary principal; assistant principal of a middle school; departmental supervisor; teacher of English and social studies; adjunct professor at Douglas College, Rutgers; and teacher of 4-year-olds in Sunday school. He received his BA from Yale, his MA from Columbia Teachers College, and his EdD from Rutgers.

An early pioneer in the use of educational technologies, he has been successful in winning major grants from Apple Computer, Commodore, and other sources, grants that were used to produce state-of-the-art multimedia labs in his last two districts. He has established educational foundations in two school districts and has successfully developed business-education partnerships.

McKenzie has published many articles and presented at many national conventions on such topics as new technologies, educational futures, site-based decision making, teaching for thinking, and team building. He is the author of two books—*Making Change in Education: Preparing Your Schools for the Future* and *Site-Based Management: A Practical Guide for Practitioners*—and he is seeking a publisher for his first novel, *Coal Creek Rebellion*.

Introduction

Despite the enormous potential of new technologies to create an educational Renaissance that would help this nation reach its goals for the year 2000, the landscape is littered with ill-considered experiments and projects that have done very little to improve student performance or change the face of education. Educational leaders can avoid this fate and develop innovative, lasting programs that produce impressive results if they pay attention to the important planning issues and strategies outlined in *Selecting, Managing, and Marketing Technologies*.

This handbook equips school leaders with a toolkit of change strategies to guide the selection, introduction, management, and marketing of new technologies so as to avoid bandwagons, premature obsolescence, and underutilization.

Selecting, Managing, and Marketing Technologies stresses the importance of clarifying the educational purposes of the school prior to the selection and purchase of equipment. Technology is portrayed as a vehicle to effect significant improvements in student outcomes rather than as an end in itself.

The key to successful implementation is effective leadership. Although the best planning results from a collaborative approach involving all key stakeholders, this committee approach is fraught

1

with perils. It can all too often end up with "the blind leading the blind." This handbook shows how to deliver innovative, forward-thinking programs with site-based decision making carefully informed by external influences to guard against what Joel Barker (1992) calls "paradigm paralysis." The leader's role in guiding the group process is instrumental and critical.

All too often, new technologies arrive during the summer and find their way into instructional areas in which the staff has been given almost no training or preparation. This handbook points out the necessity of creating an organizational culture and delivery system committed to ongoing adult learning and staff development to establish the knowledge, skill, and attitude foundation without which meaningful implementation cannot occur.

Because the process of reinventing American schools to take advantage of new technologies will extend into the next century, as today's technologies are quickly modified and improved, educational leaders must be on the lookout for expanded sources of support and funding. This handbook recommends a redefinition of the relationships of schools to external communities and shows how to parlay those relationships into expanded financial and political support for innovation.

The educational leader of this coming decade must, in John Naisbitt's words (1982), "be a facilitator rather than an order giver." *Selecting, Managing, and Marketing Technologies* is designed to help administrators, supervisors, and others facilitate group decision making regarding new technologies—so that their potential for significant school improvement can be fully exploited.

District Planning for Technology

Planning before selecting technologies can save districts a great deal of money, protect them from embarrassing mistakes, and deliver impressive educational results. Unfortunately, many schools buy equipment first and then plan as an afterthought. Assess your own district's level of planning for technology by completing the District Technology Self-Assessment Form in Appendix A. If your score comes out below 45, you will find this chapter a good place to begin making changes.

Future Perfect Planning (FPP), which forms the basis for the discussions in this book, is especially well suited to thinking about innovation. FPP is based on the work of Davis (1987), who offers it as an alternative to strategic planning, which he criticizes as being too wedded to past habits and mind-sets. Because strategic planning relies heavily on projection of trends, he argues, it is ill-prepared to help us with innovation and often hinders significant change. It does not anticipate or prepare us well for "discontinuous change," such as the breakup of the USSR.

Breakthrough technologies promise to establish entirely new learning systems, which will operate beyond the assumptions and the boundaries of the old ones. The challenge is to unleash the full potential of new technologies to support student learning, unhampered by what we might call "smokestack" conceptions better suited to a factory-based economy. FPP, whose techniques and promises are described in the next few sections, empowers a district to view the future with imagination and an open mind.

Step 1. Creation of a Planning Team

Before thoughtful decisions can be made about which technologies to purchase and how to use them, the district must clarify its learning priorities and preferences. An educational planning team comprised of teachers, students, administrators, community members, and board members should spend a year or more clarifying the mission of the district in what will be fairly simple, but compelling, terms.

Step 2. Development of Scenarios

The most important difference between FPP and strategic planning is the perspective from which each views the future. Strategic planners stand in the present and look ahead toward the year 2005, asking how present trends may twist and turn during the next decade. FPP places us in the year 2005 and asks us to imagine what learning might be like for a 7-year-old or 14-year-old. FPP encourages us to taste, smell, and see learning as the child might, free of any barriers or restrictions. After months of creating, swapping, and clarifying such images of educational futures, the planning group moves toward shared scenarios—two or three prime stories that contain the most important aspirations held by the members of the group.

Schwartz (1991) offers a five-step guide to the building of scenarios, which can serve with Davis's book as key resources to guide the planning process. He explains that scenarios are stories that help us break out of our mind-sets to see futures that might otherwise be hidden from view. As far back as 1981, prior to *glasnost*, he and fellow scenario builders at Shell Oil foresaw the breakup of the USSR using such techniques.

Appendix B is a brief educational scenario of the future describing two young girls using a hand-held computer with voice recognition to tackle a challenging social studies research task.

According to Schwartz, the planning group should pass through each of the following phases:

1. *Articulating the Current Mind-Set.* What are the key values and belief systems that have dictated behavior in the past? They are often submerged and hidden from view. Schwartz urges all members of the committee to uncover and then examine them to see if they are still valid.

2. *Hunting and Gathering Information.* Many organizations are blindsided by their tendency to gather data selectively—data that serves to confirm their old mind-sets and visions. Data that might force a reconsideration is often screened away, according to Schwartz; he recommends intentionally wandering far afield to collect items that might alert the group to the key driving forces and uncertainties mentioned next. Schools have traditionally ignored workplace realities, for example, and need to send their employees out to see how technologies are transforming the ways problems are solved and information is handled, so that they can move from the trailing to the leading edge of education.

3. *Identifying and Exploring the Driving Forces.* One way *driving forces* differ from *trends* is that they are often hidden from view, creating a stir of some kind not easily connected to the original cause. In addition to Schwartz's list, Tucker outlines 10 driving forces such as choice, life-style, discounting, and value-adding well worth the reader's time and attention, because they have great implications for schooling during this coming decade (Tucker, 1991). The planning committee's awareness of such driving forces will be instrumental in laying the groundwork for thinking about possible and likely futures.

4. *Uncovering Predetermined Elements and Critical Uncertainties.* Some factors, such as demographic trends bringing an increasingly mixed population, are essentially predetermined and highly

predictable. In the case of education, the sources of funding would be an example of critical uncertainty, as school finance suits in many states are turning the funding rules upside down and as many national leaders are pushing for school choice and the use of vouchers. The possibility of schools having to operate on a free market basis with parental choice is very real.

5. Composing a Plot. Having passed through the previous four stages, the group begins the story writing, selecting one plot from among Schwartz's list of classic plots, such as "winners and losers." It often pays, according to Schwartz, to build three scenarios, one optimistic, one pessimistic, and one in between.

Appendix C is a visualization exercise to set the scene for scenario building, and Appendix D is an example of a response to this exercise. After completing this exercise, the planning team should proceed through the phases listed by Schwartz and create the three prime scenarios mentioned in the previous paragraph. The collection of scenarios should embrace the major themes that are most important to members of the group.

Step 3. Creation of an Educational Mission Statement

In order to guide the decision making and strategies of school planners—whether in regard to technology or to curriculum or staff development—the planning team must translate its scenarios into a few brief sentences that will shape choices.

Mission statements should not be confused with board of education *philosophies*, which attempt to cover all possible goals. Mission statements focus on a few key goals that will receive special attention, and they should also clarify some process issues. Here is an example:

> The Mission Independent School District will help students become well-informed, imaginative, and effective decision makers, capable of working independently or collaboratively to create workable solutions to complex problems similar to those they will encounter during the Information Age. We will

encourage them to act in a caring, compassionate, and empathic manner. Toward those ends, we will stress activities that challenge students to do their own thinking and learning.

The reader will note that the first two sentences identify key skills and attitudes that could be translated into outcome statements and assessments. The third sentence suggests what would be a dramatic shift for many schools, an emphasis on students making their own meanings. Each district should have its own statement tied to the priorities and views of the planning group and the board of education. This statement should then work to help other, newly constituted planning groups in specific areas, such as technology, to sift through the options and possibilities that lie ahead.

Step 4. Using the Mission Statement for Technology Planning

Convening a separate group to do the technology planning, a group that also contains representatives of key stakeholders, is a good practice. It is wise to involve a cross section of people with a variety of attitudes, not just those who love technology, because it will be the responsibility of this group to help guide the entire district forward, not just the pioneers.

This group might well use the metaphor of building a Gothic cathedral to help guide its thinking and planning. No such cathedral can withstand the attacks of time and nature without solid foundations and flying buttresses, and yet the real beauty of the structure might lie in the spires stretching to the sky, in the stained-glass windows capturing wondrous images, or in the services and music contained within. A parallel situation exists with technology in schools.

Effective technology programs require electronic infrastructures analogous to a cathedral's foundations and flying buttresses. Planners must ask what kinds of electronic networks should link the students and learning centers of the schools to the rich information resources of this society, especially if one of the district goals is development of student information insight skills. They must ask what kinds of equipment will support the program they envision.

As "infotects," much like the master builders and architects of old, they must ask which elements of the foundation are most likely to withstand the tests of time and must avoid shortcuts and false economies that end up being far more costly as the system needs frequent maintenance or redesign. They must seek technology that is flexible, powerful, adaptable, and expandable.

FPP approaches to technology planning are especially well suited to questions regarding the software and learning experiences that might be supported by the electronic infrastructure. Here the planners must avoid the creation of thick, highly detailed planning and curriculum documents that can block learning, experimentation, and innovation. Once the infrastructure is in place, its use will far exceed anyone's expectations and visions, provided that a climate of responsible experimentation is encouraged by the administration.

FPP encourages open-minded planning with a focus on scenarios. The technology planning committee should spin out learning scenarios to fit new technologies—scenarios consistent with the district mission statement. These scenarios should be viewed as images of possible futures that set the basic direction but leave much room for playful program development, as the players first have a chance to use the equipment.

Step 5. Selecting and Purchasing Technologies

Building on their mission statements, some districts will design learning programs on top of their technology infrastructures, creating their own stained-glass windows and spires. They will stress the role of teacher as inventor and researcher. For such districts, the selection task is different than that facing districts who would like to buy technology and learning programs all at once. As stated earlier, the task of the latter is to install technology that is flexible, powerful, adaptable, and expandable—systems that will grow as their programs evolve; systems that will support the learning outcomes identified in the district mission statement.

A district with a commitment to student reasoning and research might put special emphasis on the development of electronic information highways, for example, linking all of the classrooms and learning centers of each building together and then linking with all kinds of information resources outside of the school, such as other schools, databases, and bulletin boards. The specific planning for how and where teachers and students will drive along the highways—the design of the program—will evolve as the system grows and driving becomes possible.

The district buying both technology and learning programs as complete packages, however, as is often the case with integrated learning systems, may find little local program invention necessary or possible. That is usually already taken care of by the curriculum staff of the vendor. Members of the planning committee must ask if they are comfortable with the way that students will be learning with the new program. How are lessons structured? What happens when a student has difficulty? What are the reward structures? How flexible and responsive is the software to individual students and their patterns? How well does the lesson sequence match the district's program? Is it drill and practice, or actually instructional?

In addition, for districts buying a complete package, members of the planning committee must also tackle the chore of sorting through the impressive claims made by many vendors, a challenge requiring some skill at comparing their evaluation designs with acceptable research standards to help distinguish between fact and fiction. The following six steps can prove helpful:

1. Ask for a *complete* list of districts that have tried the program. Sometimes the vendor might only report the most successful cases. The committee will want to hear from those who discontinued using the product as well as from those who are enthusiastic. Most ethical vendors will be forthcoming with such information.

2. Ask for written evaluation reports showing student outcomes. Some vendors hand out impressive-looking graphs that do not provide enough information to demonstrate real progress. Ask for the full story, including the sections on research design and statistical significance. If gains are statistically significant, ask how

many extra items correct that would translate to for the typical student on the standardized test. The committee should ask themselves if the dollar investment was justified by the outcomes.

3. Check to see if the evaluation design includes comparable control groups. Reviews of CAI (computer-aided instruction) and ILS (integrated learning system) evaluation studies point out that few follow the generally accepted practice of using comparable control groups—instead, studies rely on volunteers or on taking one-year "snapshots" of groups and comparing them with "expected" rates of growth. Many studies make no attempt to correct for the "Hawthorne effect," the well-known tendency for subjects of research studies to improve performance simply because they are being observed. If a serious effort was not made to hold to research design standards, it pays to ask even more questions.

4. Ask for results over a 3- to 4-year time period. Many vendors show graphs of the first year's progress; few show the long-term picture. There may be a "gadget effect" that might wear off over time. By now, ILS systems have been around long enough that committees can demand and receive such data.

5. Ask what plans the vendor has to develop new versions of the software during the next few years. What are they doing to emphasize higher-level thinking, problem solving, and student research?

6. Translate the annual cost of the hardware and the software programs into staff positions or teacher hours in staff development programs and ask which investment would do more for student learning.

When all the claims and counterclaims have been weighed and compared, the planning committee must return to the district mission statement and ask if the investment in equipment and program will deliver what the mission statement promises. The selection process must be guided primarily by that overarching question.

Step 6. Gathering Data to Steer Program Development

What you don't know may well hurt you. Informed experimentation requires the frequent and skillful collection of data in order to modify and adapt the newly implemented program. It is the responsibility of the technology planning committee to identify the key research questions worth asking, commission the evaluation design, and explore the significance of findings, suggesting program changes as data warrants.

Because few school districts invest in such data collection with regard to new technologies and the programs associated with them, they rob themselves of several important opportunities. As mentioned, the data plays an important role in building a successful program, but they can also be helpful in winning community support, gaining grant support, and maintaining credibility. Without data to show student outcomes, new technologies can too easily be characterized as frills.

Conclusion

The first decade of information technologies entering the schools has been marked by an absence of the thorough integration of those technologies into classroom life. Except in a relatively small percentage of schools and classrooms, these technologies have remained symbolic tokens of commitment to the Information Age. Numerous reports of computer usage document a general failure to blend their use into the daily problem solving and inquiry of math, social studies, science, or English classes (U.S. Department of Education, 1991). Fortunately, exceptions and models of success abound. Some districts, schools, and individuals have explored the potential of these technologies in a Future Perfect sense, casting off the limited mind-sets of smokestack education to create new ways of learning.

The challenge for schools is to achieve *breakthrough thinking*. Future Perfect Planning for technology, with its use of scenarios and its open-mindedness, offers a toolkit of strategies and devices designed to help achieve and manage such thinking.

Staff Development for New Technologies

O nce a district has completed the planning process outlined in the previous chapter, establishing clear instructional and technology program goals, it becomes feasible to define teacher competencies necessary to deliver the program. The next step is to develop a delivery system capable of establishing technological literacy and skill among the district's teachers and administrators.

Step 1. Clarification of Expectations

If a district expects widespread, broad-based, but penetrating application of new technologies, literacy and competence can no longer be viewed as a personal teacher option. A teacher for this Information Age must be literate with regard to both technology and information systems. States and districts should begin to clarify this expectation in the form of licensing, certification, and employment requirements tied to reasonable time lines.

Within a single district that has set the goal of 100% technological literacy within a 5-year time frame, the staff may be divided into two categories, each of which will deserve a different approach regarding literacy and skill:

1. New Hires. Clearly defined teacher competencies should be established as criteria for selection and hiring of staff. The more that institutions of teacher training see such criteria being applied to their graduates, the better job they will do of equipping their students with such skills prior to graduation. A wise district will save itself considerable training expense and gain program momentum by requiring all new hires to arrive technologically literate and skilled. These new hires should then be asked to commit to a program of maintenance and skill updating, much like that required of doctors who must contend with rapidly advancing technologies and treatments.

2. Regular Staff. All staff members who are likely to remain for 5 or more years should be required to attain technological literacy within that time period in order to maintain employment, but the district must provide the learning resources these staff members require to gain such literacy. Each teacher should make a formal commitment to a learning program personally designed from the district's offerings. Once literate and skilled, the teacher should proceed to maintain and extend those levels of proficiency in subsequent years as the technologies grow and develop. The creation of a strong staff development program as outlined in the next section will be a costly venture, but the costs of inaction will be greater as they appear in program obsolescence and teacher ineffectiveness.

Step 2. Creation of a Staff Development Planning Committee

The most effective programs will emerge from a planning committee with strong staff participation combined with staff development expertise based on research on effective practices. The goal is to create a 5-year adult learning plan with many different options and opportunities to match the diversity of styles and needs that exists within the ranks of any school district.

When this committee has completed its planning and program invention, staff members should be able to page through a booklet outlining a 5-year progression of learning opportunities and make selections customized to fit individual preferences and needs. The committee will then continue to meet and adjust the program over the succeeding years, as data is collected to assess the effectiveness of the offerings.

Step 3. Design of Program Offerings

Findings from research on effective staff development programs from Joyce and Showers (1983) and others should be blended with research on adult learning to design offerings that maximize success and progress while developing an appreciative and enthusiastic response to the new technologies. Here are some guidelines for design:

Guideline 1. Programs should provide options suited to the different learning styles of participants.

Not all teachers should pass through the same courses or the same types of courses. Some may prefer to learn various software packages in some version of independent study, with an advisor or tutor or help-line available to assist when problems are encountered. Others may prefer small study groups. Still others may desire formally structured classroom instruction, with a linear progression through carefully defined objectives with plenty of guided practice and support. It makes no sense to force adults to participate in a learning experience that conflicts with the way they learn best.

Guideline 2. Programs should provide substantial opportunities for staff members to practice the new technologies as they will actually be used within their own classroom learning situations.

Many existing staff training models introduce technologies to teachers in generic terms. Math, social studies, English, and science teachers often find themselves mixed together. Although this strategy may serve well enough to introduce the fundamentals, it is essential to move on to subject-specific situations and opportunities so teachers can see, touch, and feel the applications as they relate to the teachers' own assignments. Not transferring new technology programs to regular classrooms has been a major cause of failure of these programs in the first decade. Strategies to support such successful transfer must be a high priority in the creation of staff development programs.

Guideline 3. Time for the staff to learn new technologies should be provided on a paid basis by the school district.

Unlike many corporations that typically dedicate substantial budgets to pay for employees to learn new skills and new technologies, schools have all too often relied on the individual teacher's goodwill and dedication to support training programs. Teachers are often expected to attend sessions on their own time after school, during the evenings, and on weekends. If teacher pay were on a high professional level, that might be a reasonable expectation; but it is time districts showed commitment to training by paying for it. Without such payment, reliance on volunteers makes it difficult to ever reach the 100% technological literacy goal.

Guideline 4. Instruction should be designed with the comfort and the attitudes of learners in mind as well as the cognitive and skill objectives.

Too much instruction in the use of technologies fails to address the substantial anxiety felt by many people as they first try driving a videodisc player with a computer or test out some other new piece of equipment. Learner comfort and user friendliness are key issues in instructional design that deserve formal attention. The coverage of too many skills or too much material in too short a time can only be achieved at the expense of staff support for the introduction of these technologies to their own classrooms.

Guideline 5. Staff development should be defined broadly to include any meaningful way that teachers might acquire the technological literacy and skills identified by the district.

Visits to other schools, peer coaching, visits to the workplace, graduate courses, and many other experiences should fall under the staff development umbrella and receive due consideration by the planning committee. How well is the district utilizing each of these experiences? Can changes be made that will multiply the benefits of each? Can the district's tuition reimbursement program be modified to encourage attention to technologies, for example?

Guideline 6. School district administrators should be expected to achieve technological literacy along with the rest of the staff.

If administrators hope to lay claim to the title of *technology leaders,* they must establish a comfortable relationship with the technologies that are likely to shape much of the classroom learning that will be taking place during the coming decade. As outlined in the next chapter, it will be their role to support the rest of the instructional staff in their journey toward full integration.

Guideline 7. Instructors for the staff development program should be selected from a broad cross section of the teaching staff, not a narrow segment with a special affinity for technology.

In order to avoid overreliance on the technologically savvy individuals or on the math and science departments, districts should invest in the development of instructors from across the disciplines who may bring a variety of teaching styles, attitudes, and approaches to the learning experience.

Guideline 8. The program should provide support groups and ongoing help-lines to maintain continued growth.

The path to natural and automatic use of an innovation is often lined with obstacles, disappointments, and frustrations. Joyce and Showers (1983) and others have documented the powerful effects of allying learners with partners who will provide the support necessary to keep the learner moving forward. Because schools and classrooms can be isolating, new communication systems can do a great deal to bolster the courage of novices, letting them know that help is just a phone call away and the phone is just a few feet away.

Guideline 9. The technology program should be thoroughly integrated with the rest of the district's staff development program so that technologies are seen as delivery systems to complement other instructional systems.

One hypothesis to explain the low level of program integration during this first decade of microtechnologies is the tendency for administrators to establish staff development programs that show the staff how to use the machines (to type a paper, for example) but not how to employ them instructionally.

Guideline 10. The program should provide opportunities for participants to demonstrate mastery, literacy, and competence.

In order to comply with a district mandate for 100% technological literacy, there must be provision for the valid and reliable assessment of learner proficiencies. The well-crafted program provides for multiple pathways, but learner outcomes should be clearly defined and measurable.

Guideline 11. The program should require all staff members to develop some awareness of the change literature as well as develop a toolkit of innovative thinking skills and group decision-making skills.

Because innovative programs usually bring with them some degree of pain, loss, and difficulty, teachers must be schooled in the realities of change. Developing a tolerance for the frustrations accompanying the inevitable changes of the coming decade should be of the highest priority.

Unlike many school programs, most new technologies cannot be simply purchased and installed. In most cases, they are not the whole program in themselves but merely a set of tools to support development of a program. Teachers will be expected to develop classroom applications and guide students in the innovative use of the technologies. To achieve such levels of inventiveness, teachers will require the skills of both researcher and curriculum inventor. Program invention will very likely require a kind of collaborative, team effort for which many teachers are at the moment ill-prepared.

Early experiments with site-based decision making demonstrate the need for extensive training in group process so that the staff can work effectively together to define and solve problems. Most groups benefit from work on consensus building, active listening, and structured decision making.

Step 4. Adaptation of the Program

Once the program is under way, the staff development planning committee gathers data on a frequent and continuous basis to evaluate progress and adapt the program. The committee also keeps an eye on the horizon, so that fast-breaking new developments can be rapidly embraced and incorporated into the program. With the introduction of some new technology—such as Apple's Newton, for example—the committee is quick to consider its significance for the school district and to begin planning for its arrival. The committee is responsible for making certain that the program remains dynamic, flexible, and current.

Conclusion

Effective and widespread use of technologies in schools requires an immense investment in staff learning. School districts must do more than provide a series of courses; they must establish a culture within their districts that promotes continuing learning as a norm for all staff members. Administrators must move toward the kinds of structures and learning teams envisioned by Senge (1990), who sees members of the organization on a quest for change and improvement, continually asking how life can be made better.

The School Administrator as Technology Leader

School administrators play a critically important role in developing successful technology programs. Leadership may be the keystone without which the full arch cannot stand. Because many schools rely on the heroic efforts of individual technology enthusiasts, efforts that are generally not coordinated by any central figure, technology implementation is too often spotty and inadequate. We need fewer heroics and more systematic innovation.

The central metaphor I will use for the administrator's role as technology leader is that of the master gardener supervising a team of highly skilled gardeners with mighty green thumbs. This master gardener inspires the team to complete the following functions with imagination and spirit:

Cultivating the Soil

Schools are often tradition-bound, caught in time-honored patterns of behavior that are deeply embedded and resistant to challenge or review—they are often set in their ways. If innovation of any kind, technological or curricular, is to occur, the soil must be loosened and turned over. The administrator tills the soil, employing the tools of organizational development to identify and initiate the cultural changes that are required to support innovative thinking.

Although innovation requires frequent communication and idea swapping, most schools isolate their teachers. They work in separate rooms and see little of each other throughout the work week. Time is not available to support idea swapping and generation.

The effective administrator pushes the system to create free time, by either strategic scheduling, the use of substitutes, or some fancy rule bending. She or he also uses effective questioning as a spade to free the organizational soil of rocks and clods that might inhibit growth or learning. Questions put old mind-sets out on the table for reexamination. The administrator asks others to provide answers, trusting the soil, carefully prepared now, to generate healthy crops. The goal is the development of an organization that welcomes the planting of new ideas.

These days, we hear a lot about organizations such as schools challenging and changing old paradigms or ways of doing things. Barker (1992) suggests replacement of old paradigms with new ones, but we are moving into a period of time when no single paradigm will serve us well. More likely, organizations will need "flexadigms," flexible ways of thinking capable of bending and twisting to match the demands of a turbulent and surprising world. The task before the school administrator is to support the staff in the development of such a flexadigm so that schools are in a state of constant renewal, change, and growth. Rigidity, decision making by formula or recipe, and reliance on standard operating procedures are anachronistic.

Fertilizing, Watering, and Providing Light

Just loosening up the organizational soil is not sufficient, of course. The technology leader breaks down the traditional isolation of schools from outside resources by inviting a rich flow of ideas and possibilities into the school.

Acknowledging that schools have not afforded most staff members opportunities to know and appreciate the innovations taking place elsewhere in the nation, even within their own building or district, the leader works to expand those opportunities by bringing more ideas into the school and by encouraging the staff to visit or investigate other programs. Because some staff are cut off from professional reading and research, the leader encourages them to create a professional library in each school and makes certain that key journals and articles circulate freely and frequently. All staff are encouraged to keep an eye out for relevant articles and circulate them when they find them.

In addition to a rich flow of ideas, the leader waters the soil by providing a steady stream of new skills and learning experiences that will deepen and extend the staff's innovation toolkit. The leader becomes a staff developer now, working to expand the knowledge base regarding technologies and the decision-making skill base. With the support of the administrator, each staff member develops an annual professional improvement plan that states personal growth objectives in the areas of instructional strategies and new technologies. The administrator, knowing the objectives of each staff member, makes a concerted attempt to match opportunities to objectives. Staff development becomes a daily occurrence rather than a yearly event.

Fertilizing and watering must also be accompanied by sunlight—the administrator making certain that efforts are carefully assessed using formative evaluation—the gathering of data during a technology program in order to adapt and steer the program toward optimal performance. Too many school innovations have failed because participants believed, "What you don't know can't hurt you."

The leader makes certain that the team asks the right questions and collects the right data, both quantitative (numerical) and qualitative (descriptive). The goal is the creation of an organization that is reflective in its practice, continually asking: "What's happening? How might we change what we are doing to improve results?"

Collection of data is often viewed with suspicion by staff members, who have concerns that the data might be used in an evaluative manner to assess their own performance. The mere hint of accountability raises eyebrows and defensiveness in many districts. In order to avoid such a reaction, the administrator makes certain that the staff members have a strong voice in the design of a study and in the collection of the data, providing appropriate training in formative evaluation so that they can see the benefits of data collection for program adjustment and development.

Seeding

To plant a garden, we often need more seeds than will ever germinate and become mature plants. Technological innovation in schools is similar. The leader makes sure that the building staff can select from a rich menu of program options, software, and equipment, counting on the staff to further expand the richness of these possibilities by adding their own insights, their own variations, and their own signatures to the original versions.

The leader becomes a technology resource manager, careful to plant seeds where they are most likely to grow. Knowing the quirks, strengths, and personalities of all staff members, he or she carefully targets certain individuals for particular opportunities. Sometimes it may require a word of encouragement or some coaxing. Other times the recipient will pounce eagerly.

Basic to this function is the leader's responsibility to keep an eye on the horizon, always scanning for new ideas, new software, new equipment, new programs, and inspirations of any kind. To mix metaphors a bit, the leader climbs up the mast to the crow's nest and tries to see around the earth's curves. The leader also encourages other staff members to look for great ideas, whether it be the media specialist or a classroom teacher. The more who are on the lookout, the better.

Along with the rest of the staff, the administrator establishes a web of idea-collecting mechanisms and nets—subscribing to many journals, participating in computer bulletin boards, attending technology-oriented conferences, developing networks with similarly inclined school leaders, and mining the rich resources available through online databases that allow one to store *alerts*, which are standard searches repeated monthly on various topics of high interest to the school. If videodiscs are a priority, for example, the leader can automatically receive a listing of current articles as they roll off the press and into the databases. Once ideas are collected, however, the discussion and consideration of those ideas must be organized.

Connecting Rows for Irrigation

As mentioned earlier, the isolation of teachers in their classrooms and a lack of time for meeting and planning in groups has contributed mightily to school stagnation. The administrator must emphasize staff connectivity in every way possible to guarantee cross-fertilization, pollination, and irrigation. There will come a day when every staff member has a hand-held computer such as Apple's Newton to carry around in school and at home, which will make such staff connectivity and communication omnipresent and omniscient. In the meantime, leaders must establish whatever formal and informal networks they can within the resources that exist, recognizing that the workday schedules of teachers usually conspire to block communication and idea swapping.

Simply structuring more time for meetings and exchanges is not enough. As mentioned in Chapter 2, the staff must possess group process skills so that meetings are productive and innovative in nature. In many schools where the culture has not been particularly collaborative in the past, the staff must be shown how to explore ideas in a nonadversarial manner, using what Senge (1990) calls "dialogue" rather than discussion. Otherwise, in the words of one observer of site-based decision making, they are "like newly freed East European countries suddenly faced with solving massive problems" (Brandt, 1992, p. 3).

Weeding

Just as not everything growing in a garden is worth keeping and just as some plants and weeds can draw nutrients away from the real crop, some technology experiments will prove unsuccessful, undesirable, and worthy of elimination. The administrator must play a central role in helping the staff develop evaluation criteria to guide decision making—some programs must be pulled up by the roots so that others can thrive and grow. This is not to suggest an arbitrary wielding of power by an individual. The key element is the set of collectively established criteria that can be used to judge the effectiveness and value of experiments in an objective manner.

Once again, the value of data collection and formative program evaluation is clear. Implementation without such evaluation data throws the school into risk, because it will be difficult otherwise to distinguish between hybrids on one hand and weeds on the other.

Inoculating Against Disease and Warding Off Pests

Computer viruses are not the only kind of disease from which an administrator must protect the system. The more complex the systems linking classrooms and delivering services, the more vulnerability. The administrator keeps a watchful eye on the systems, providing adequate security for files, proper ventilation and cooling, alarms to guard against theft, and public relations efforts to keep critics and naysayers from undermining the integrity of the effort. In keeping with the stress on collaboration, the administrator makes this a shared responsibility, engaging staff members in protecting the integrity of their own program, encouraging all to be public relations spokespeople. Dirty laundry belongs only at the meeting table where it can be handled constructively and positively.

Rotating Crops

The wise leader makes sure that the opportunities and responsibilities associated with innovation are spread around and rotated in such a way that there is equity—that no one group or individual is overloaded or treated with favoritism. Overreliance on a few heroes and pioneers may weaken the overall success of the innovation, creating resentment as well as harmful schisms and cliques.

Pruning

Even good programs, like bushes and trees, can benefit from careful and timely pruning. In conjunction with research data, the administrator leads the team in asking what changes need to be made in the original plan. What elements should be eliminated, cut back, or modified? This function also suggests that programs are more likely to thrive if they are not allowed to grow too fast and too large. Sometimes success is a program's own worst enemy, as pressures mount to expand beyond the system's capacity to function with quality.

Planning for Fallow Fields

A constant diet of innovation and turbulent change can leave staff members weary and resistant to any further suggestions. The leader has the responsibility to support a reasonable pace for change and to provide times when the fields may rest fallow and regain their strength. The leader encourages the group to keep an eye on organizational resilience. The use of technology in schools is an "ultramarathon," not a sprint.

Grafting

Some programs with limited or moderate promise may become superior programs if merged with the elements of other programs. The leader is always on the lookout for such combinations and is quick to support the combinational thinking of team members. Creativity and innovation is often a matter of rearranging the parts of what already exists in novel ways.

Conclusion

Some critics argue that because school administrators have little training in the kinds of leadership outlined in this chapter, school restructuring has little chance of succeeding: "Ideas such as vision and developing shared leadership are quite beyond most of those who occupy administrative positions in our schools" (Tye, 1992). The competencies required by school leaders in the coming decade are quite different than they were during the smokestack era:

- Setting direction
- Organizing and implementing
- Monitoring
- Communicating
- Developing staff
- Managing relationships
- Adapting actions to context (after McCauley, 1990)

Although the challenge of creating appropriate leadership may be enormous, we have little choice. The time has come to make such proficiencies a matter of certification and licensing, just as this book calls for information and technology literacy as a job require-ment for teachers. And just as teachers deserve 3 to 5 years to "get up to speed," this generation of school leaders deserves a grace period during which they can acquire the skills they might have missed during their years of earlier training. As with most profes-sions today, educational leaders and staff workers alike must be in a constant state of renewal in order to keep up with the rapid rate of change.

Winning Community Support
for Technology

Successful technology programs of the coming decade must establish strong linkages with a widening community. Leaders recognize that an extensive investment in equipment and software requires a firm foundation of external support and a broadened conception of community. In addition, schools must do a better job of marketing services to traditional client groups.

The health and future of school district technology programs may rely increasingly on the thoughtful cultivation of powerful constituencies hitherto neglected or ignored. Because the proportion of taxpayers with students in the public schools may drop to levels as low as 20% in many places, schools cannot expect to maintain funding unless some action is taken to reach a broader group. The funding of anything perceived as innovative or supplementary becomes problematic during times of scarce resources (McKenzie, 1991b).

Some portions of this chapter were adapted with permission from the December 1991 issue of *From Now On*.

Marketing Versus Sales

Schools must begin marketing technology programs and indeed programs of all kinds. What do we mean by *marketing*? As opposed to sales, marketing requires listening and learning whereas sales emphasizes persuasion. A school leader emphasizing a marketing approach begins by identifying all clients and potential clients of the school. He or she would then learn everything possible about the preferences, likes and dislikes, and needs of these clients.

The next step is to bring services in line with what is learned so that they match needs. Even then the leader may not rest, for it still remains to alert the clients—including the nontraditional groups newly identified—to the match between these services and their interests. When the school leader successfully awakens enthusiasm for school services in the area of technology, she or he soon finds groups that had previously considered schools off-limits now using schools.

In the past, when districts worked with the public in the field of education, the districts had a tendency to adopt the sales model of persuasion. Having a product in which they believed, the districts saw their task as convincing the public—and a fairly narrow public at that. This chapter explores the potential of using marketing strategies to strengthen relationships with both the traditional client base and the potentially new clients alluded to earlier.

New Clients and Market Niches

To broaden the client base, districts must look for market niches ignored in the past. They might begin by reexamining and challenging many of the underlying assumptions that characterize schooling—with what Barker (1992) calls a "paradigm shift."

The old *paradigm* (assumptions, rules, and boundaries) governing schooling included the following beliefs in many districts:

- Schools are for young people between the ages of 5 and 19.
- Schools open in the morning and close in the afternoon.
- Technology programs are for young people.

What if the following notions were introduced as substitutes?

• Schools are for all townspeople.
• Schools—like ATMs—are open at all hours they are needed.
• Technology programs are for all townspeople.
• School leaders are marketing maestros.

As Tucker (1991) demonstrates in his book on driving forces of change, changing demographics have great significance for schools. Those school districts that focus all their energies on a shrinking client base—the group Tucker calls "the baby bust"—risk starvation and decline. Dividing the population into three main groups ("waves")—the mature market, the baby boom, and the baby bust—Tucker points out the following:

• People over 65 are the fastest growing segment of the U.S. population.
• People over 50—25% of the population in 1990—are the most affluent consumer group in history. The 50-plus age group controls two-thirds of the net worth of all U.S. households and accounts for 40% of consumer spending.
• People over 55 purchase 80% of all luxury travel in America (Tucker, 1991, p. 67).

At the same time this mature group is growing in numbers and purchasing power, the youngest part of the population—the traditional school clientele—has been shrinking. The other main group, the baby boomers, continue to grow in power and affluence as they age: "The number of households headed by those between 35 and 54 will grow by 50% by the year 2000" (Tucker, 1991, p. 67).

Schools might seize on this information as an opportunity and ask how they might serve the interests of the mature market and the baby boomers with a technology program.

Reaching the Mature Market

Begin with research. Districts should find out everything they can about the mature group, taking the time to identify their leaders, to meet with individuals, and to ask many questions. How do they like to spend their time? What are their interests? How can the district's technology program match those interests and needs?

Note the emphasis on travel by this group. Is that true in your district's community? If so, all kinds of valuable services can be offered by showing members of this group how to make use of telecommunications to make airline reservations and to comparison shop.

Redefine school hours so that the mature market can gain convenient access to the technology. Open the school media center to the community several nights each week and on Saturday mornings. Run classes showing people how to use the official airline guide (OAG) to explore plane schedules. Take advantage of the electronic information services available through databases such as DIALOG and CompuServe. Develop an inexpensive little flier that can be included in the same envelope with quarterly tax bills: "Next time you are planning a trip . . . " Make it clear that the district technology is available for use by the mature market.

Gather the organizational leaders of the mature market together and discuss communications. How are they creating and distributing their newsletters for various clubs and groups? Do they have access to desktop publishing and database software to print mailing labels? If not, run classes and teach them how to take advantage of these technologies. Provide convenient access to the technology throughout the week so they can benefit from their investment of tax dollars. Why should they have to buy computers, scanners, and laser printers when they can be available from 4:00 p.m. daily?

Is the mature market in your town politically active? Do they follow legislation in Washington or your state capitol? Why not run courses on how to track legislation through the various database services?

Does this group enjoy investing in the stock market? Do they have investment clubs? Are they familiar with the many services offered by Dow Jones? Here is another potential series of classes.

How about communicating with people around the country and the world? If this group loves to hop into a van or RV and tour the country, why not show them the myriad bulletin boards available on GEnie and CompuServe? Before they leave on their trip to New Mexico, they can develop electronic friendships with people from that region who can suggest great restaurants, spectacular views, and traffic patterns worth missing.

Does the mature market have a strong interest in continuing education? Would your distance-learning technology help provide evening or daytime classes especially suited to this group?

Do they appreciate electronic arts and crafts? One way to convince this group that these technologies are powerful tools of invention and expression is to sit them down for 10 sessions with *Adobe Illustrator* or *Aldus Freehand*. Take them far enough into the software so they feel its power. Scan a photograph and show them how to modify it with *Photoshop*.

Introduce them to the magic of CD-ROM and videodiscs. Let them dance through Shakespeare's collected works or visit the Louvre. The mature market are powerful consumers. Show them the advantages of comparison shopping by computer.

Gather the leaders of the mature market together and share information about Apple's grants of equipment to community groups. Offer to help write the grant proposal.

There is a tremendous amount of technology power going underutilized each day in schools across the land. After millions of dollars are invested in wonderful equipment, it sits unused for 16 hours each day. Some studies have shown that many computers, especially stand-alones in classrooms, are dark even during class hours. If we could rethink our utilization patterns, we could double the availability of the hardware—for students as well as for the adults in the community.

If students do not have home computers, how do they write term papers and essays? Do the wealthy students have an unfair advantage? By keeping labs open in the late afternoon and some evenings, we serve the mature market, the baby boomers, and the students all at the same time. As a side benefit, we begin to build community across groups at a time when groups are segmenting and separating. We begin to heal the divisions that so often show up at election time.

Reaching the Baby Boomers

How does a district broaden its marketing campaign to include the baby boomers and all other important constituencies? We can replicate many of the same strategies used for the mature market, beginning, for example, with the leadership of important groups throughout the community.

Hold a coffee meeting for the officers of all clubs, service organizations, and associations within the community. Many of these groups will be paying a premium for the design of newsletters, for mailing services, and for printing. Show them how they can cut those expenses by more than half by taking advantage of school equipment. Open the doors on a regularly scheduled basis during the business day and in the evenings so that businesspeople and others can work side by side with students.

The advantage to the small business or club of using school hardware is the lowering of costs without investing big dollars. Such small users may decide to purchase an inexpensive computer to compose their newsletters, but it will save them quite a bit to rely on school equipment for high-quality printing, scanning, CD-ROM storage of graphics, and the like.

This chapter cannot anticipate all the useful strategies that might be designed to match the special needs and interests of the groups in a district's community. That can best be done by the school leader's asking key questions and doing some serious listening.

The important thing to remember about this marketing approach is that your district's understanding of client needs and interests must be updated on a frequent basis. Decades of practice have accustomed schools to the notion of steady states, conditions during which all systems operate smoothly with little adjustment and with high predictability. Those days, if they ever existed, lie behind us. School leaders must use at least five strategies to maintain current understanding of client needs:

1. Surveys of attitudes, preferences, and needs
2. Individual interviews
3. Focus groups
4. Informal observation

5. Scanning of the horizon for new developments, trends, and driving forces

Reaching the Traditional Client Base

Using some of the marketing strategies listed above, most schools could dramatically improve services to students and their families while strengthening their community support base for further exploration of technologies.

Schools might begin their marketing with questioning that taps client needs and attitudes broadly and then might focus in on ways to deliver technology programming effectively. For too long, schools have acted as if their clients are captive and have no place to go. In many cases, the strategy of developing school programs without "catering" or "pandering" to client needs and interests has been couched in professional philosophies and values. With justification, many educators feel that some parents can and do make poor decisions for their children and that it is the job of educators to protect children from such bad influences, whether it be the parent who pushes too hard, the parent who neglects, or the parent who abuses.

The challenge is to pose the right questions to find out how both students and families are feeling about key issues and then to create programs that meet those client needs that reasonably match district values.

Once committed to marketing, a school staff might discover the following situation through questioning: The parents would be much happier if the school day extended from 7:00 a.m. to 6:00 p.m., so they would be able to cover their work responsibilities without worrying about taking care of their children. The staff might reasonably complain that the parents are too little committed to nurturing their children and that the schools are being forced into baby-sitting.

At the same time, the nation's economy and the nature of work may have changed so dramatically that these parents feel they have little choice other than having both parents work long hours, and they will seek alternative care for their children regardless of how the school responds to their needs. In many cases, a single parent is struggling to raise a family on a limited income and cannot afford the luxury of greeting the children at 3:30 with milk and cookies. The response to this client need might be an extended school day, which would be educationally and socially preferable to a hodgepodge of informally created baby-sitting alternatives.

Marketing surveys are available to help schools begin this questioning process (McKenzie, 1991b). If those surveys fail to touch on key concerns, each school may add items to fit local circumstances and technology issues. Appendix E offers an example of a marketing survey that supports questioning with regard to technologies.

In most districts, there will be substantial numbers of parents who do not understand how new technologies might be central to the education of a child for citizenship in the next century. They may have too little personal contact with such technologies in their own workplaces to understand their significance. At the same time, the schools may not have been using technologies in ways that are analogous to workplace applications. One of the goals of a marketing campaign is to bring parents into more active contact with the new technologies so that they gain a personal appreciation for the power of these technologies to enhance decision making, communication, reasoning, and performance.

Ameritech has launched an exciting experiment, Project Homeroom, with high schools in the Chicago area, which provides hundreds of families with home computers to link teachers, parents, and students via Prodigy. With this hands-on opportunity, parents begin to see the dramatic ways the new technologies may shift communication and learning.

The school's marketing should include students as well as parents, because many schools have inadvertently fallen into patterns that make existing technology more available or more attractive to some groups than to others. In many schools, patterns of use reflect gender, race, socioeconomic status, and preferences for various subjects such as math and science. In order to change these patterns to achieve broader acceptance of new technologies by students, schools must take the time to gather data and question their students.

If we find that young women in our high school spend far less time than young men using computer labs outside of school hours, for example, we need to ask them why that might be so. Our questioning may uncover social reasons that can be addressed through some form of new club or organization that reverses the trend and makes it socially acceptable for young women to visit the labs after school. For further help in this specific area, Eldredge (1990) has assembled a solid research base on strategies that can be used to close the gender gap in technology.

Each school will face challenges unique to its setting, but if a school invests in understanding its traditional client base and developing technology program designs to meet client needs and interests, the resulting support foundation will amply repay the school staff for the time invested.

Conclusion

School leaders must redefine their job assignment to include marketing campaigns that will broaden community involvement and support for technology programs—or the coming decade will be one of declining resources and disappointment. Schools also must redefine their missions to include all learners within the community, consciously pursuing and courting each of the three age waves. We must learn from the dinosaurs' example and adjust our behaviors before the arrival of conditions that could cause our extinction.

Identifying New Sources of Funding for Technology

For many years, the philanthropic world virtually ignored K-12 education, but the good news is that conditions are improving to some extent as many businesses are becoming increasingly concerned about education. Now the enterprising school district can significantly expand technology programs by identifying and pursuing alternative funding sources, many of which have been overlooked in the past. To some extent, the race will go to the swift, as the pool of available resources is not likely to expand greatly in the near future.

School Leaders as Grantwriters and Grantseekers

Although many school administrators might rightly argue that they already have a full plate managing their buildings and current assignments, changing financial conditions now require a

---

Sections of this chapter were adapted with permission from the September 1991 issue of *From Now On*.

change in role so that innovation can thrive. Because few districts can afford to hire individuals with grantwriting expertise, all school leaders must become proficient in the resource-hunting game.

Winning grant support is most likely when funding is requested for a program that is impressive and innovative yet practical and readily transferred to other districts and schools. Successful grant-seeking and grantwriting, therefore, depend on the generation of worthwhile and inventive solutions to real school challenges. The school leader is responsible, as noted in Chapter 3, for creating an "educational hothouse" that produces many such great ideas.

There are two basic strategies for program funding. One approach begins with the program invention and then identifies a donor likely to support such a program. The other approach starts with a donor's request for proposals (RFP) and develops a program in response. Each is valid, and each thrives when an invention team is called together under the administrator's leadership (McKenzie, 1991a).

Big Fish in a Small Pond: Selecting Funding Targets

In 1989, a fellow school administrator returned from a state-sponsored workshop on applying for vocational-education funding to announce that the state was allowing only 3 weeks for districts to create and submit proposals and that nearly everybody left the meeting grumbling that they had no intention of complying with such an impossible time frame. We saw their grumbling as an opportunity that we might become a "big fish" in a small pond and managed to win more than $150,000 for our small district by quickly assembling a dynamite proposal.

In the past, most school districts have restricted grant writing to major foundations and governmental programs, and those proposals have been focused on the most highly publicized RFPs. As a result, the competition has often been brutal and the rewards limited. The major premise of this chapter is that efforts are most likely to pay off when the district is able to identify funds for which there is relatively little competition or when the district is able to distinguish itself from the crowd of grantseekers by the quality and the marketing savvy of its proposals .

Although it is not a waste of time to search through grant announcements in sources such as *Education Week*, because those RFPs are also the best known by the rest of the educational world they are the most competitive and least likely to pay off.

At least one or two members of the administrative team should learn how to conduct database searches, which will greatly improve the targeting of donors. Databases can expedite the treasure hunt in remarkable ways. DIALOG, for example, offers three databases that could prove very useful in identifying educational venture capital. If your district does not already subscribe to one of these database services, the investment of a subscription may reap a great harvest. You may contact DIALOG at 800-334-2564.

Here are three databases accessible through DIALOG:

1. *The Foundation Directory* (cost = $60 per hour of search time) is a comprehensive directory providing descriptions of more than 25,000 grantmakers, including grantmaking foundations, operating foundations, and corporate grantmakers. This database can be searched by many of the elements in a record, identifying all foundations located in your state that contribute more than $ 75,000 annually, for example. It can also be searched by zip code to find all foundations within your own community. There can be some very big and pleasant surprises using zip codes—the "needle in the haystack" may prove to be a very large family foundation that happens to reside right in your own backyard. Each record provides address, telephone, key contacts, geographical areas funded, and the size and types of grants made each year.

2. *The Foundation Grants Index* (cost = $60 per hour of search time) offers more than 440,000 records since 1973, outlining the kinds of grants awarded by more than 400 major American philanthropic foundations. Information on grants given by the foundations is useful in determining types and amounts of grants awarded, because foundations seldom announce the availability of funds for specific purposes. Word searches can be performed to find which foundations have made grants in areas such as "science" and "the arts."

3. *Grants* (cost = $60 per hour of search time), provided by Oryx Press, Phoenix, AZ, contains more than 8,200 records and is updated monthly. *Grants* lists thousands of RFPs offered by federal, state, and local governments, commercial organizations, associations, and private foundations, with application deadlines up to 6 months ahead.

Careful mining of these resources can provide your district with a remarkable competitive advantage in the grantseeking game.

The Importance of Forming an Educational Foundation

Although responding to RFPs is an important and worthwhile strategy, the most fruitful sources of new funding require the establishment of a district educational foundation, which will provide tax benefits to donors who otherwise might not donate funds to the public schools. The rest of this chapter shows how to identify those new sources of funds that will flow to the accounts of the newly formed educational foundation.

By creating a district nonprofit foundation, contributions may be made on a tax-deductible basis by both individuals and businesses. The foundation must be incorporated under the laws of your state and forms must be filed with the IRS listing the foundation as a nonprofit foundation. Because each state's requirements for foundations will differ somewhat, it is wise to create your foundation by collecting the bylaws and filing papers of half a dozen other foundations already established by districts in your state. The IRS publishes detailed booklets explaining how to complete its forms. Legal advice should be sought during this process, but the least expensive route is to cut and paste other districts' documents and then ask for a review from an attorney.

Bylaws and Board Policy Issues

Although foundations may be established by boards of education with some overlapping membership, the IRS requires a significant level of independence. When reviewing models from around your state, it is important to note the sections defining membership on the board of the new foundation. Are the interests of the board of education adequately protected by the selection process?

Because there is some danger that foundations might try to force programs and values on a school district that are in violation of community preferences, many foundations have it written into their bylaws that they may only solicit funds for school projects listed and approved by the board of education in advance. They may not dream up projects of their own. This provision helps the school district and its professional staff maintain control.

Another issue worth tackling in the bylaws is the role of the foundation's board. It usually works best to focus the board on its policy functions and to create a small executive committee charged with carrying out the business of the foundation in between quarterly meetings. The actual work of the foundation should be conducted by a team of school district administrators charged with operating responsibility.

Board Membership as a Strategic Tool

The members of the foundation board can be valuable resources as the district begins its treasure hunt. The school administrator and the board of education should begin by identifying the 4 or 5 largest national or state corporations with facilities within your school district territory or the region nearby. Each of these companies should be invited to nominate a member, hopefully an executive with a student in your schools, to the board of the new foundation. It works best if the superintendent and the board president have lunch with the facility manager and explain the purposes of the new foundation before pitching membership on the board.

In addition to representatives of big business, there should be 2 to 3 members who are influential in the local chamber of commerce, individuals who can establish good contacts for the foundation with the local businesspeople. There also should be several board members who work professionally in the fields of grantwriting, fund-raising, development, or foundations who can provide excellent strategic advice. Finally, there should be several members who are well-connected with parent and community groups of various kinds. Careful selection can pay great dividends further down the road.

Promoting Foundation Programs

Once the foundation is established and the school district has decided the kinds of programs that will be funded, it is time to develop a public relations campaign combining news releases with carefully developed promotional literature describing the projects deserving venture capital. Local public relations and printing professionals may be willing to donate valuable services to the foundation in support of this effort.

Identifying and Pursuing All Potential Technology Supporters

Because there are many potential donors who are never asked to support school ventures, many school districts are a bit like orchards with fruit rotting on the ground. The first step after forming the foundation is to develop an inventory of local possibilities and then begin working to contact them to request their ongoing support.

Large Corporations

This target has already been discussed to some extent in the earlier section on selecting board members. The goal is to sign up each of these major corporations for at least a $10,000 annual, repeating contribution so the foundation can count on some $50,000 to $75,000 or more revenue each year.

It is important to distinguish between corporate funds that are routinely budgeted for community relations and those that reside in corporate foundations at the national level. The district should go after both sources, but your foundation should be primarily interested in the community relations funds that most facility managers can invest each year without consulting the national headquarters, because these are the funds least sought after by other school districts. In many places, schools have *never* asked for a share of these funds, but many facility managers are pleased to donate as a basic cost of doing business in a town.

Business leaders see contributions as an investment in goodwill that will pay dividends whenever the company needs to deal with local government in the guise of the planning board or other agency. The main strategy here is to request a 5-year commitment to fund some program such as staff training in new technologies and to provide the company in return with much publicity as well as a seat on the foundation board. Each successful partnership will require skillful courting by the superintendent and board president.

The district may also seek funds from a corporation's national foundation, knowing that many of these foundations give preference to proposals from organizations where their corporate facilities are located, and the key here is to work with the local facility manager, winning her or his endorsement for the proposal and asking for assistance in moving the proposal through the corporate bureaucracy.

Small Businesses

This is another major source of funding that often goes untapped by school districts. The secret to reaching this group is the development of some kind of broad-based campaign that signs up doctors, lawyers, accountants, retail merchants, and various other kinds of businesspeople as continuing donors and provides some kind of ongoing public recognition of their role as school district patrons. If several hundred agree to donate $250 each year, the district can add another $50,000 to the $50,000 mentioned earlier.

It also pays to identify benefits that might accompany patronage, along the lines of frequent traveler programs. Because training of employees will become an increasingly pressing issue for small businesses during this coming decade, for example, patrons might be extended access to classroom and technology resources outside of the normal school day, as a cost-free courtesy. Each district should work with its small business contacts to determine just which package of benefits might prove most appealing.

Alumni

Private schools invest a good deal of energy in maintaining close contact with alumni, involving them in major capital campaigns and ongoing support programs. Districts should imitate their model, recognizing that many of their alumni work for companies that will match their employees' donations. Districts should also identify alumni who have been especially successful and give them an opportunity to express their gratitude for their good start in life.

Parents

Given the anti-spending climate that emerges in many communities because the great majority of taxpayers do not have children in schools, parents may have to take a more active role in supplementing school budgets than they have in the past. As with alumni, it pays to develop two different types of campaign, one that is broad-based and aimed at all parents and one that is targeted directly at the most successful and affluent families.

Bequests

Some people reach the end of their years without any family members or worthy causes to which they might leave their estates. Lawyers who handle bequests indicate that this is a group worth identifying and courting, and it need not be wealthy individuals. Every once in a while a newspaper carries the story of a retired classroom teacher who leaves $75,000 to the local school district. A few such bequests each year would bring the district's new revenue above the $250,000 mark. The strategy here is to identify the attorneys in town who routinely handle estates and ask for their advice. It might pay to print up a special brochure from the foundation explaining why and how one might leave an estate to the school district.

Marketing Technology Proposals: Packaging and Persuading

Many solid guides to grantwriting are available—from organizations such as the Foundation Center in New York—that describe how to put together each section of the grant proposal. This section stresses several strategic approaches not usually found in such guides, but it is still recommended that school leaders consult such sources to learn the basics.

Know Your Target

Many grantwriters pay too little attention to audience. The more one knows about a particular company or foundation, the more successful one can be in shaping the proposal to be appealing. Using a database, one can find out what kinds of grants they have made, what rules and time frames they have, what kinds of programs they really care about, and what style they like. It usually pays to call the organization and request a copy of their annual report, because that document clarifies guidelines, grant criteria, and philosophy. Meeting with a representative prior to drafting the proposal, in order to ask questions and test the waters, is a wise approach. At all costs, avoid the "blind date" approach to grantwriting.

Standing Out From the Crowd

Outstanding grant proposals are remarkable in several ways; they demand attention and respect. The school leader will want to differentiate his or her proposal from the pile of requests that the funding organization routinely receives.

The Goal

Start with an idea that is noteworthy and unique—the kind of idea that will raise eyebrows. This idea should show up in the opening section, which clearly states the project goal. It should be startling in its originality and its simplicity. The reader should remark, "That's a great idea! Why haven't other people thought of that before?"

The Need

Make the need for your program dramatically evident by presenting strong evidence. Too many grantwriters rely on platitudes and generalities. If you wish to close the gender gap, present numbers that document the problem in stark terms. Always supply data.

Existing Research

Demonstrate how your proposal pushes practice beyond what has already been done by reporting the results of your ERIC search conducted online to review up-to-the-minute literature and research reports. If you wish to employ multimedia as part of a social studies program to counter what Toffler (1990) calls "infotactics," show your potential donor that no one else has ever tried what you are proposing.

Measurable Objectives

When translating goals into objectives, make certain that every objective contains within it a standard by which growth and change can be objectively measured, so that the donor knows what they may accomplish. If trying to close the gender gap, for example, state: "Enrollment by female students in technology-related courses will climb from its present 35% to 48% within the 3 years of the project."

Clear Writing

Many grantwriters make the mistake of thinking that complicated and jargonistic language will impress the donor, but the reverse is usually true. The kind of prose that passes for writing in most graduate schools of education is unduly jargonistic and abstract. Most readers will be more impressed by clarity and concise prose. In fact, many corporations and foundations prefer a 2- to 3-page letter to the 50- to 60-page documents often required by the government. They want to know in simple terms what it is you propose to do and why you think their investment in your program will pay great dividends.

Persuasive Writing

Districts need to take a few lessons from Madison Avenue, noting that persuasion touches the right side of the brain in order to stimulate appetites of one kind or another. Unfortunately, much of most school leaders' formal training in writing has overemphasized abstraction and so-called objective and dispassionate prose. On occasion, it is helpful to blend into the grant proposal anecdotes, stories, and words that appeal to the senses and emotions. Here again, though, it pays to know your audience. If the foundation is quite stuffy in its formal communications, it may be wise to write in a stuffy manner. If they are more playful and poetic, it is wise to mirror their preference.

Appetizing Packaging

Within reason, good taste, and the rules of the foundation, a grantwriter may help a proposal stand out by changing the format in various ways. Consider printing the proposal on colored paper of a slightly different size than 8½ x 11—it will then always be more visible. Print the proposal itself with 3 to 4 different colors, even if you have to pay for professional output because your district does not own a color printer. Demonstrate your technological savvy by incorporating computer-generated graphs and graphics to substantiate your case. Send along a *HyperCard* or *Persuasion* version of your proposal to accompany the hard-copy version. One successful grant application to Commodore several years back included jelly beans in the mailing package with the grant proposal, playing on the "computers for human beans" advertising theme being employed by the computer company. Recognize, however, that there are risks to such strategies and that it pays to know the audience. *Outstanding* should not mean standing out in the cold.

Compelling Evaluation

Many philanthropists complain that giving money to schools often seems like pouring money down the drain, because it is hard to see results when the project is finished. If the grantwriter can develop an evaluation design that addresses this concern, the proposal will have a definite competitive advantage. Involve professional program evaluators in helping you design this section.

Impressive Staff

Many organizations will want to know why your project team can be trusted to pull off such an ambitious project. Make sure that the résumé of each participant is tailored to fit the project. A résumé is too often a generic document used in job searches, and it may contain little information to show why the individual has the skills, the experience, and the know-how to support a great project. Supplementing the project team with representatives from business and graduate schools who are interested in supporting the project is a wise move.

Conclusion

Scarce resources will impede school districts' ability to explore new technologies unless we find new sources of funding for innovation. It is unfortunately true that innovation is usually the first part of a school budget to be cut during hard times. School leaders who wish to remain on the cutting edge will become treasure seekers, reaching out to build an impressive group of educational stockholders—people and organizations willing to invest in our nation's future by supporting innovative school practices. Given the nature of the global economy, supporting schools is becoming the patriotic thing to do.

Appendixes

A. District Technology Self-Assessment Form

Answer each question with one of the following choices and then use the number beside each choice to evaluate your answers:

Excellent (5)
Good (4)
Fair (3)
Weak (2)
Poor (1)

1. Is there a sense of purpose? Is there a plan?

Related Questions: Is there a written district technology plan that clarifies philosophical commitments and directions for district staff? Does this plan focus on the horizon, on the long view? Does it leave room for steering and flexibility as staff learns through experience? Does it address all critical elements of program implementation, including staff development as well as hardware purchases? Is the plan research-based? Were all key constituents involved in creating the plan?

2. Is the technology being used?

Related Questions: Does the district have some method to quantify or track the percentage of time that equipment is being used by students or community members? Is there a system to figure out which staff members are making use of the equipment and which are not? Does the administration and the board take a position with regard to computer and technology usage? How much usage would be desirable—100% of the school day? 75%? 65%? 35%? Is there a gap between desired and actual usage? Does anyone know why? Is there a staff plan to narrow the gap?

3. Is technology blended into regular classroom learning?

Related Questions: If technologies are basic tools for managing information in the Information Age, they should be used broadly, within the art classrooms, the English classrooms, the vocational classrooms, and all others. Studies of schools have shown that technology usage is often centered in special niches and departments, such as a computer department or the media center, and that the usage is often concentrated in the hands of a narrow group of pioneers or champions. Are appropriate uses of technologies written into all of the district curriculum documents as mandatory activities to prepare students for the next century? Do all subject teachers make use of online databases, CD-ROM discs, and word processing for research projects, for example? Do students learn to create multimedia reports? If your district uses computer-assisted instruction (CAI) or an integrated learning system (ILS) approach, how closely are those learning experiences dovetailed with their corresponding subject areas? If a child is doing reading practice on the computer, will it be on the same skills as she/he is developing with the rest of the language arts program? Is the new technology an organ transplant that has been accepted, or is it a grafted limb being rejected?

4. Does the use of technology mirror workplace realities?

Related Questions: Has your district explored how adult workers are currently using technologies to do scientific research, writing, planning, designing, evaluating, and the like? Has that exploration been translated into school experiences and programs? Is technology thought of primarily as a teaching tool or as a problem-solving tool of everyday life? How well are the school technology experiences preparing students for the Information Age workplace? Is there an explicit district definition of the Information Age? Is the staff aware of how the use of information is transforming work and the kinds of skills required by today's workers? Has Toffler's *Powershift* (1990) been carefully reviewed? Was Carnevale's *Workplace Basics* (1988) from the American Society for Training and Development considered? Are technologically savvy representatives of the profit and nonprofit sectors consulted when the district does technology planning?

5. Is the staff adequately prepared to use the technology?

Related Questions: Has the board funded a comprehensive staff development plan over 3 to 5 years or more to provide all teachers with sufficient technology skills to implement an appropriate program? Are all teachers required to acquire such skills? Are assessment plans in place to determine what course offerings need to be added in future years? Does staff development take place during the regular work year/day or is it added on in ways that require teachers to subsidize the learning with volunteered time? Is compensation for training/learning reasonable and fair?

6. Does the staff ever visit the workplace?

Related Questions: What provisions are made for staff members to spend time in the modern workplace seeing how technologies are employed? What percentage of English teachers, for example, have spent a day in a modern newspaper office seeing how technologies support the writing, design, layout, and production of a newspaper? How many science teachers have visited a modern science lab to see how computers may be used to conduct experiments and model scientific phenomena? How many media specialists have visited modern libraries offering cutting-edge information systems?

7. Is access to technology equitable?

Related Questions: Does the district monitor technology usage by gender, race, location, and academic track to make certain that access is equitable? What kinds of data are collected and reported to help guarantee equal access? When evidence arises that there are gaps of various kinds, what provision is made to close such gaps?

8. What kinds of relationships should students have with machines?

Related Questions: Has the board expressed community values in concert with the professional staff with regard to desirable relationships between students and machines? Are these values communicated explicitly in board policy or in a district technology plan? How much time should students be engaged with various kinds of technologies? Who should be in control, the student or the machine? What are the long-term consequences of such relationships? How do they relate to other educational goals such as citizenship and self-esteem?

9. What implicit values are taught by technologies?

Related Questions: Is there a system in place to review the implicit values or hidden curriculum taught by various technologies? If computer software rewards students for correct responses by providing game time or opportunities to blow up aliens, for example, is such a reward system consistent with board policies and community values? Does the technology stress extrinsic or intrinsic rewards? Is responsibility for reviewing such issues clearly identified? Is there a board policy regarding software piracy and violations of copyright? Do students see ethical behavior modeled by the professional staff? Are ethical issues related to technologies addressed by curriculum areas such as social studies? Are students taught critical thinking and critical viewing skills to equip them to counter propaganda and media distortions? Will they emerge from schooling as thoughtful consumers or impulsive consumers? Will they be passive viewers or active viewers?

10. Does the technology enhance self-esteem, independence, and imagination?

Related Questions: In *Workplace Basics*, a need is stated for workers who know how to learn independently, come up with novel solutions to problems, and ride through the turbulence of a changing economy and society with self-confidence and adaptability. Are district technology experiences designed to deliver that kind of work force? How do you assess progress toward such goals? Do you measure student self-esteem, independence, and imagination? Is there a program review process to determine which learning experiences are most likely to promote the growth of such qualities?

11. Is the technology more effective than alternative strategies?

Related Questions: Is the technology the only way to provide a particular learning experience such as mastering various reading skills? If not, does the technology deliver results that are superior to corresponding alternatives for a comparable investment? If a district chose to invest in staff development aimed at improving teachers' reading instruction, for example, would students in those classrooms make smaller or larger gains than those in classrooms where an ILS system was installed? Does the district introduce such programs as pilots allowing for compare-and-contrast reviews of costs and benefits? Is the data from such studies made available to the board as part of the district decision-making process?

12. Is the district evaluating what is happening?

Related Questions: What kinds of data are gathered to assess the impact of various technologies? Is the data gathered in an objective fashion following accepted principles for experimental design to avoid bias? Does the evaluation design take into account issues such as the Hawthorne effect and the differential impact of volunteers as implementers of pilot programs? Is data used formatively, as a guide to future decisions and program modifications?

13. *Is the technology efficient, flexible, adaptable, and current?*

Related Questions: Are issues such as processing speed, expandability, and connectivity addressed in district planning and purchasing? If students will be using the technology to do graphics or CAD, for example, do cost considerations result in the purchase of low-speed technology that will require students to sit and stare at the screen for minutes at time, wasting thousands of hours over the course of a year? Do similar considerations result in the purchase of black-and-white monitors, which limit the ability of students to work in 3-D or work with multiple variables in graphing and statistics programs? When videodisc players, CD-ROM players, computers, video cameras, and the like are purchased, are choices made with a 3- to 5-year perspective? Are models with maximal expandability and adaptability selected to protect against premature obsolescence? Is obsolescent existing technology maintained far past program usefulness because it has not stopped working or broken down? What planning procedures are in place to provide for timely updating of technologies and the transfer of obsolescent equipment to programs in which the shortcomings are irrelevant?

Total Score ____
55-65 = Outstanding
45-55 = Strong
45 or less indicates a need for improvement

B. A Future Perfect Scenario

In this scenario, we explore what learning might be like in the future, with highly intelligent hand-held computers acting as tutors and learning assistants.

Amy and Nakisha, two middle school students, arrive with a team of classmates at the archeological dig site and proceed directly to their assigned square, designated by a grid of string stretching across the remains of what used to be an Iroquois longhouse.

"Where did we leave off yesterday?" they ask Joe, their hand-held computer.

A smiling face appears on the small screen and provides directions. "You were carefully removing soil from your square when you ran out of time. One of your brushes had begun to uncover what looked like a pottery fragment."

The girls nod their heads and bend down close to see if they can still make out the outline of the fragment. "There it is!" exclaims Nakisha, excitedly. She begins brushing around the piece with great care as she has been taught to do by Joe's careful tutoring. As several inches of surface are freed of dust, a faded painting (perhaps of flowers?) begins to emerge.

Amy holds Joe close to the fragment so the computer can scan the image. "Take a look at this painting, Joe, and tell us what you can."

Joe's scanner goes to work and quickly reproduces the image from the pottery shard to its own screen. After a few moments, Joe reports that several similar pieces were located in nearby squares just that morning by two other teams.

"Can you let us see all of the pieces together?"

The girls stare at the fragments and then begin to move them around on the screen like pieces of a jigsaw puzzle, only the computer allows for a 3-D effect. Gradually, the pieces begin to take on the look of a water jug.

"Can you clean this up and show us from your memory images of other similar pieces found at other sites?"

The girls peer down at the screen and watch the fragments being rearranged, merged, and then brightened on the screen before them. The computer shows them what looks like a freshly made jug with a decorative ring of brightly painted flowers. Another five similar pieces appear in a brief slide show narrated by Joe, who explains which tribe created each piece and what features were unique to each piece or tribe's work.

"Can you date this for us, Joe, and get a hold of our teacher for us so we can report our findings?"

Mrs. Grimm's face appears on the screen with a grand smile. "Great work, girls! You have added another important piece to the puzzle. Go right ahead and finish the removal of your fragment, following the normal procedure for labeling, boxing, and storing. Send a message to the nearby teams so they can profit from your findings. I'll see you in class tomorrow."

Both girls smile proudly as they bend down to finish their work.

C. Visualizing the Future

Instructions: Imagine that you are a student in the year 2005. As you learned from the Future Perfect Scenario, in this future time the environment and conditions for learning may be very different from what they are today. The nature of the learning experience is limited by your imagination. Close your eyes and try to picture, smell, and feel what learning might be like. After 5 to 10 minutes, write each of the following sentence starters at the top of a page of composition paper and respond to each, listing as many ideas as possible:

1. I feel _____
2. I will _____
3. They will _____
4. I am _____
5. I can _____

D. Visualizing the Future—Sample Response

1. I feel curious, alive, full of wonder, encouraged, intrigued, overwhelmed, at risk, alive, supported by my peers, like dancing, like whooping it up, like jumping high, like moving on. I feel confused, abandoned, alone, lost, at risk, on the edge, but alive. Curious and alive.

2. I will go inside to find a book, to find an answer, to finish a project, to check the oven, to take a trip. I will start a voyage to another land, see the land, speak with another child, ask many questions, hear answers, develop understanding, solve the puzzle before me and start another.

3. They will ask me to explain, question my thinking, applaud my performance, suggest new strategies, coach, model good inquiry, listen, learn from me, cry when I move them, hug me when I need it, let go when I am ready.

4. I am scouting frontiers, asking questions, surrounded by questions, inventing answers, testing answers, on my own but part of a team, challenged but supported, pushed beyond simple recipes, intrigued, trying out new poses, new possibilities, afraid of the truth, afraid of the lie, committed to the truth, undone by the lie, willing to dare, to take a risk, to leap tall mountains, to find something better.

I am an actor, a dancer, a potter, a poet, a scientist, a tinkerer, a tailor, a cabinetmaker, a mommy, a daddy, a friend, a neighbor, a scout, an inventor, an architect.

5. I can smell flowers, feel the sun on my neck, touch the grass, chase a butterfly, sing songs, learn from my friends, play, jump and skip, hear stories, explore, fall down, skin my knee, sketch the geese in flight, hear laughter, see joy.

E. District Technology Marketing Survey

Dear Parent:

In an effort to develop school programs to match the real needs and interests of our students and their families, we are conducting this survey to learn more about your involvement with the new technologies that are becoming an important part of our society. Your answers to this survey will help us create technology plans for the school district, which should lead to improved services.

1. Please indicate which of the following types of equipment you currently own at home:

( ) Personal Computer   ( ) Dot Matrix Printer
  Brand _____ ( ) Laser Printer
  Model _____ ( ) Modem
( ) Compact-Disc Player (music) ( ) Videodisc Player
( ) Compact-Disc Reader (text) ( ) Scanner

2. Do you presently subscribe to any of the following online information services?

( ) Prodigy ( ) Dow Jones ( ) CompuServe ( ) DIALOG
( ) Other _____

3. Which of the following are frequent home uses of your equipment?

( ) Games & Entertainment   ( ) Home Business
( ) Desktop Publishing   ( ) Databases
( ) Graphics   ( ) Spreadsheet
( ) Word Processing   ( ) Tax Programs
( ) Telecommunications   ( ) Research
( ) News

4. Which pieces of technology would you like to purchase next?

_____

_____

5. If we could make this kind of equipment available at one of our schools for community use, would you take advantage of the opportunity?

( ) Definitely yes   ( ) Perhaps   ( ) Unlikely

6. In which field are you employed, and which technologies do you use in your place of work?

_____

_____

7. Would you be willing to conduct a career exploration workshop for students showing them how these technologies have changed your job?

( ) Yes   ( ) No

8. What technology skills would you like to learn if the schools could provide instruction through an adult-education program?

_____

_____

9. How would you rate the job our schools are doing equipping your children with technology skills and awareness?

A ___   B ___   C ___   D ___   E ___

10. What have we done involving your children and technology that seemed especially worthwhile?

_____

_____

_____

_____

_____

11. What have we failed to do with technology that we ought to be doing?

_____

_____

_____

_____

_____

12. How could we improve our educational services regarding technologies?

_____

_____

_____

_____

_____

13. How many children do you have at each level of the district?

Elementary ___
Middle ___
High School ___

14. How many years have you lived in this town? ___

Annotated Bibliography and References

Annotated Bibliography

Barker, J. (1992). *Future edge: Discovering the new paradigms of success.* New York: William Morrow.

Provides a clear overview of the way that paradigms often serve to block change and adaptation in organizations faced with turbulence. Profiles various figures such as paradigm pioneers. Offers strategies for organizational success in making the paradigm shifts required by new conditions.

Carnevale, A. (1988). *Workplace basics: The skills employers want.* Alexandria, VA: American Society for Training and Development.

Outlines major skill areas required for successful competition in a highly technological, global economy, including the importance of learning how to learn, working in teams, negotiating, and solving problems creatively.

Davis, S. (1987). *Future perfect.* Reading, MA: Addison-Wesley.

Offers an approach to planning that supports freedom from old mind-sets and a more open-minded perspective than traditional strategic planning models. Shows how this approach is better suited to managing discontinuous change.

Finkel, L. (1990). Moving your district toward technology. *School Administrator Special Issue: Computer Technology Report*, pp. 35-38.
Outlines do's and don'ts that will help a district move toward increased technology use in schools. Areas covered are teacher training, computer access, computer location, leadership, and technology plans.

Fullan, M., & Miles, M. (1992). Getting reform right: What works and what doesn't. *Phi Delta Kappan, 73*(10), 744-752.
Advises that instead of developing a new strategy for each reform wave, educators must learn how to foster continuous improvement. Reforms often fail because of faulty maps of change, complex problems, overreliance on symbols, superficial solutions, misunderstood resistance, attrition, and misuse of knowledge. Success means recognizing change as a systemic, resource-hungry, locally inspired journey into uncertainty and complex problem solving.

Glickman, C. (1992). The essence of school renewal: The prose has begun. *Educational Leadership, 50*(1), 24-27.
Warns that the growing acceptance of school restructuring efforts may prove dangerous as advocates enact sweeping proposals without the proper grounding in a set of principles developed by the participants. Expresses concern about bandwagon effects.

Hanson, E. (1991). *Educational marketing and the public schools: Policies, practices and problems.* Riverside, CA: California Educational Research Cooperative.
Explains how marketing relates to public schools and how schools may develop marketing mechanisms to draw schools and their communities into productive and supportive relationships.

Herman, J., & Winters, L. (1992). *Tracking your school's success: A guide to sensible evaluation.* Newbury Park, CA: Corwin Press.
Offers a practical approach to qualitative and formative program evaluation in order to guide school change efforts. The approach is especially suited to site-based planning groups without much formal evaluation expertise.

Joyce, B., & Showers, B. (1983). *Power in staff development through research in training.* Alexandria, VA: Association for Supervision and Curriculum Development.

Outlines the characteristics of staff development programs that have been proven effective by research. Provides models for the creation of district programs.

McCauley, C. (1990). *Effective school principals: Competencies for meeting the demands of educational reform.* Greensboro, NC: Center for Creative Leadership.

Advances a list of competencies that school leaders will need during the coming decade in order to meet the kinds of changes schools will be facing. Explains the importance of each skill.

Schwartz, P. (1991). *The art of the long view: Planning for the future in an uncertain world.* New York: Doubleday Currency.

Makes a case for scenario building as a planning strategy to prepare organizations for uncertain futures. Provides a step-by-step outline of how to proceed.

Sydow, J., & Kirkpatrick, C. (1992). Inject reality into your technology planning. *School Administrator, 49*(4), 31-33.

Presents a technology-planning framework for administrators that facilitates development of a strategic plan. The process includes planning the planning, benchmarking the current status of district technology use, envisioning future trends, identifying stakeholders' needs and wants, developing the technology model, identifying resource requirements, and developing a strategic plan of direction for creating detailed annual tactical plans.

Toffler, A. (1990). *Powershift: Knowledge, wealth and violence at the edge of the 21st century.* New York: Bantam Books.

Describes how influence is shifting to those nations with the largest percentage of brainworkers, as the ability to manage information has become the preeminent source of power in the global village. Suggests that schools must radically alter their missions to prepare young people for such a future.

Tucker, R. (1991). *Managing the future: 10 driving forces of change for the '90s.* New York: Putnam.

Explains 10 driving forces—such as life-style, convenience, techno-edge, and quality—that have become major factors in winning market share. Shows how companies can thrive by addressing these forces in their strategies.

References

Barker, J. (1992). *Future edge: Discovering the new paradigms of success.* New York: William Morrow.

Brandt, R. (1992). Building community. *Educational Leadership, 50*(1), 3.

Carnevale, A. (1988). *Workplace basics: The skills employers want.* Alexandria, VA: American Society for Training and Development.

Davis, S. (1987). *Future perfect.* Reading, MA: Addison-Wesley.

Eldredge, M. (1990). Gender, science, and technology: A selected annotated bibliography. *Behavioral & Social Sciences Librarian, 1,* 77-134.

Glickman, C. (1992). The essence of school renewal: The prose has begun. *Educational Leadership, 50*(1), 24-27.

Joyce, B., & Showers, B. (1983). *Power in staff development through research in training.* Alexandria, VA: Association for Supervision and Curriculum Development.

McCauley, C. (1990). *Effective school principals: Competencies for meeting the demands of educational reform.* Greensboro, NC: Center for Creative Leadership.

McKenzie, J. (1991a). The art of the deal—no trump: Grantwriting and educational foundations for difficult times. *From Now On, 2*(1), 3-15.

McKenzie, J. (1991b). The art of persuasion: Marketing new technologies to key constituents. *From Now On, 2*(4), 3-8.

Naisbitt, J. (1982). *Megatrends: Ten new directions transforming our lives.* New York: Warner Books.

Schwartz, P. (1991). *The art of the long view: Planning for the future in an uncertain world.* New York: Doubleday Currency.

Senge, P. (1990). *The fifth discipline: The art and practice of the learning organization.* New York: Doubleday Currency.

Toffler, A. (1990). *Powershift: Knowledge, wealth and violence at the edge of the 21st century.* New York: Bantam Books.

Tucker, R. (1991). *Managing the future: 10 driving forces of change for the '90s.* New York: Putnam.

Tye, K. (1992). Restructuring our schools: Beyond the rhetoric. *Phi Delta Kappan, 24*(1), 8-14.

U.S. Department of Education. (1991). *The state of mathematics achievement: NAEP's 1990 assessment of the nation and the trial assessment of the states.* Washington, DC: Author.